Bengaluru Brunch

A collection of South Indian Recipes

Chaya Gopalan

Written with
Jyothi Kudva

Bengaluru Brunch

Published by : Chaya Gopalan
St. Louis MO, USA
Email : bengalurubrunch@gmail.com

First Edition @ 2012

Printed and Designed by :
Tejas Printers, Bangalore
tejas.printers25@gmail.com

Preface

Food makes one feel happy and cooking relieves stress which is especially true for me. Raised in a family with a tradition of rich Indian food, I was drawn into cooking at a young age in order to help my mother prepare many of these dishes. Compiling recipes by tasting wonderful food has become a habit and many friends and relatives contribute to this growing collection—a tradition of sharing that has been instilled in my cooking. My daughter started writing recipes even before she could spell words correctly! Her being far away from home and her perpetual requests for our family recipes has inspired me to put the recipes in the form of this book. These recipes are modified to meet the taste of my own family or due to the difference in the nature of the ingredients available in another country. Although brunch was not something I grew up with, having lived in the US, I thought of collecting only those dishes that would be appropriate as brunch items as my focus in this book. The majority of the brunch dishes included here are from the Southern region of India.

Table of Contents

Starters

Entrees

Curries and Stir Fry Dishes

Avalakki Chuda

(Spicy Flaked Rice)

Flaked rice – 1 cup

Peanuts – ½ cup

Cashews – ½ cup

Curry leaves – 1 tbsp

Garlic – 4 cloves crushed

Dry coconut pieces – ½ cup

Roasted split chick peas – ½ cup

Red chili powder – 1 tsp

Asafetida – a pinch

Turmeric – ¼ tsp

Cumin powder – ¼ tsp

Oil – for deep frying

Salt – ½ tsp

Method

Deep fry the flaked rice, peanuts, cashews, curry leaves, dry coconut pieces and garlic scparately. Mix together and add the chili powder, asafetida, cumin powder, turmeric, roasted split chick peas and salt. Mix thoroughly.

Ground Meat Kachori

(Ground Meat Stuffed Pastry)

Filling:

Prepare the ground meat filling as on page 42

Shells

All-purpose flour – 1 cup

Fine semolina – 1 tbsp soaked in 1/3 cup water

Rice flour – 1 tbsp

Oil – for deep frying and an extra tbsp

Salt – a pinch

Method

Mix in the all-purpose flour, rice flour, oil, salt, and the soaked semolina into a soft dough. Form 1-inch balls, flatten and roll into thin circles. Place 1 tbsp of the filling in the center, gather the edges and press to seal. Pinch off the any extra dough and deep fry.

Hurigalu

(Baked Bean and Peanut Snack)

Pigeon peas – ½ cup

Black chick peas – ½ cup

Black eyed peas – ½ cup

Dry green peas – ½ cup

Peanuts – 2 cups

Roasted split chick peas – ½ cup

Dry coconut pieces – ½ cup

Red chili powder – 1½ tbsp

Curry leaves – 2 tbsp

Cumin powder – ½ tsp

Lemon juice – 2 tbsp

Asafetida – ¼ tsp

Salt – to taste

Method

Soak the beans overnight in separate containers, drain and pat dry on a kitchen towel. Bake each bean type separately in a single layer at 350°F for 50 minutes and the peanuts for 30 minutes, while stirring occasionally. Dry curry leaves by microwaving for approximately 1 minute and crushing.Mix the red chili powder, cumin powder, salt, curry leaves, asafetida and lemon juice. Mix in the beans and peanuts. Add coconut pieces and roasted split chick peas.

Khara Biscuit

(Spicy Biscuit)

All-purpose flour – 4 cups

Butter – 2 sticks softened

Sugar – 1½ tsp

Cumin – 1 tsp

Curry leaves – 1 tbsp chopped

Cilantro – 2 tbsp chopped

Ajwain – 1 tsp

Green chilies – 10 chopped

Baking soda – ¾ tsp

Yogurt – 6 tbsp

Salt – 1½ tsp

Method

Mix the butter, sugar, cumin, curry leaves, cilantro, ajwain, and green chilies. Fold in the all-purpose flour, baking soda and salt. Add in the yogurt and knead gently into a soft dough. Form 1-inch balls, flatten gently and bake at 325° F for 40 minutes or until golden brown.

Kodubale

(Spicy Rice Rings)

Rice flour – 3 cups

All-purpose flour – 1½ cups

Asafetida – ¼ tsp

Cumin – 1 tbsp

Sesame seeds – ¼ cup

Grated fresh or dry coconut – ½ cup

Red chili powder – 1 tbsp*

Butter – 1 stick softened

Water – 1¾ cup warm

Oil – to deep fry

Salt – 1 tbsp

Method

Mix the dry ingredients together along with the butter. Drizzle in warm water and knead into a soft dough. Pinch off about a tea spoon of dough and shape into a ring. Deep fry on medium heat until golden brown.

*Red chili powder can be replaced by 8 green chilies chopped fine, 1 tbsp chopped cilantro and 1 tsp grated ginger.

Kosambari

(Lentil and Cucumber Salad)

Split green gram lentils – ½ cup

Cucumber – 1 cup grated

Carrots – 1 cup grated

Green chilies – 2 chopped

Red chilies – 2 broken

Black pepper corns – 1 tsp crushed

Fresh coconut – 1 tbsp grated

Lemon juice – 1 tsp

Mustard seeds – ½ tsp

Cilantro – 2 tbsp chopped

Curry leaves – 1 tbsp chopped

Asafetida – a pinch

Oil – 1 tsp

Salt – to taste

Method

Soak the lentils in water for 3-4 hours. Drain and mix with the cucumber, carrot, green chilies, coconut, lemon juice, curry leaves, crushed black pepper and cilantro. Heat the oil and add mustard seeds. When they splitter, add the red chilies and brown. Cool to room temperature and stir into the mixture above. Add salt just before serving and mix well. Garnish with chopped cilantro.

Masala Kadale

(Spicy Peanut Snack)

Peanuts – 3 cups

Chick pea flour – 1 cup

Rice flour – ¼ cup

Red chili powder – ½ tsp

Asafetida – 1/8 tsp

Cumin powder – 1/8 tsp

Oil – for deep frying and 1 tbsp hot

Water – ¼ cup

Salt – ½ tsp

Method

Roast peanuts in the oven at 350°F for 15 minutes. Mix the chick pea flour, rice flour, salt, cumin powder, asafetida and red chili powder with water into a thick paste. Add the roasted peanuts, the reserved oil and mix well. Fry in hot oil in batches until crisp.

Mirchi Bonda

(Banana Pepper Fritters)

Banana peppers – 4 halved

Split chick pea flour – 1 cup

Rice flour – ¼ cup

Red chili powder – 1 tbsp

Baking soda – ½ tsp

Water – 1 cup

Cumin powder – ¼ tsp

Oil – for deep frying

Salt – to taste

Method

Mix the flours, red chili powder, baking soda, cumin powder, and salt. Add the water until it has reached the consistency of pancake batter. Dip each cut pepper in the batter and deep fry on medium heat until golden brown.

Muruku

(Spicy Rice Curls)

Rice flour – 1½ cups

Split chick pea flour – ½ cup

Butter – 1/3 stick softened

Cumin – 2 tsp

Roasted split chick pea – 2 tsp powdered

Ajwain – 1 tsp

Red chili powder – 1 tsp

Baking powder – ¼ tsp

Water – ¾ cup and 1 tbsp warm

Oil – for deep frying

Salt – to taste

Method

Mix the dry ingredients along with the butter. Drizzle in warm water and knead gently into a soft dough. Fill a Muruku Machine with the dough and press directly into the hot oil. Fry until golden brown.

Muruku Press

Nippattu

(Spicy Wafers)

Rice Flour – 3 cups

Split black gram lentil flour – 1/8 cup

Split chick pea lentils – ¼ cup Soaked and drained

Oil – for deep frying and 1 tbsp hot

Curry Leaves – 1 tbsp chopped

Chili powder – 1 tbsp

Water – 1 3/4 cups

Salt – to taste

Method

Mix all the dry ingredients together along with 1 tbsp hot oil. Drizzle in the water and knead gently to form a firm dough. Form 1–inch balls, flatten on a plastic sheet (such as Ziploc Bag or a cereal bag) and deep fry until golden brown.

Pakoda

(Spicy Fritters)

All-purpose flour – 1cup

Rice flour – 1½ cups

Split chick pea flour – ½ cup

Red chili powder – 3 tbsp

Onions – 2 cups grated

Garlic – 2 cloves thinly sliced

Green chilies – 6 chopped

Cilantro – ¼ cup chopped

Asafetida – a pinch

Cumin powder – ½ tsp

Coriander powder – ½ tsp

Cashews – ½ cup chopped

Oil – for deep frying and ¼ cup hot

Salt – to taste

Method

Mix everything together with the hot oil to form a dough. Pinch off ½ - inch balls of dough, flatten and drop into the hot oil. Deep fry on medium heat until crispy.

Spicy Roasted Nuts

Almonds – 1 cup

Walnuts – 1 cup

Pecans – 1 cup

Cashews – 1 cup

Red chili powder – 1 tbsp

Oil – 3 tbsp

Lemon juice – 1 tbsp

Cumin powder – 1 tsp

Asafetida – 1/8 tsp

Salt – 1 tsp

Method

Roast the nuts separately in the oven until crispy (cashews, peanuts and walnuts take about 20 minutes, almonds take approximately 30 minutes). Mix the chili powder, asafetida, cumin powder, oil, salt and lemon juice in a large bowl. Add the roasted nuts and mix well.

Dahi Vada

(Lentil Fritters in a Yogurt Sauce)

Split black gram lentils – 1 cup

Baking soda – ¼ tsp

Cilantro – 1 tbsp chopped

Paprika – ¼ tsp

Water – 2 tbsp and a bowl of hot water

Yogurt – 3 cups

Salt – to taste

Oil – for deep frying

Method

Soak the lentils for a minimum of 4 hours, drain and grind with the water in a food processor stirring often. Mix in the salt and baking soda. Form 1- inch balls and flatten on your wet palm. Make a hole in the center, slide into the hot oil, and deep fry until golden brown. When done, drop the fritters into a bowl of hot water. Drain on a paper towel, arrange in a layer or two in a shallow dish. Spoon yogurt over the fritters. Sprinkle salt and paprika over the top and garnish with the chopped cilantro.

Maddur Vada

(Spicy Crisp Pancakes)

Fine semolina – 1 cup

All-purpose flour – 1 cup

Rice flour – ½ cup

Oil – for deep frying and ¼ cup hot

Onion – ½ cup diced

Green chilies – 8 finely chopped

Cumin powder – ¼ tsp

Asafetida – 1/8 tsp

Cilantro – 2 tbsp chopped

Curry leaves – 1 tbsp chopped

Water – ¾ cup

Salt – to taste

Method

Mix semolina, all-purpose flour, rice flour, ¼ cup hot oil, onion, green chilies, cumin powder, asafetida, cilantro, curry leaves, salt and water together and knead into a firm dough. Form 1-inch balls, flatten on a plastic sheet (such as a Ziploc bag or a cereal bag) and deep fry until golden brown.

Masala Vada

(Spicy Split Chick Pea Fritters)

Split Chick pea lentils – 2 cups of dry lentils soaked overnight and drained

Garlic – 6 cloves

Ginger – 1–inch cube

Green Chilies – 12

Cilantro – 1 cup

Mint – ¼ cup

Dill (optional) – ¼ cup

Curry Leaves – 1 tbsp

Onion – 1 cup diced

Fennel seeds – 1 tsp

Cloves – 20

Cinnamon – 2 sticks

Salt – to taste

Oil – for deep frying

Method

Chop the garlic, ginger and green chilies coarsely in a food processor. Add the cilantro, mint, dill, curry leaves and continue to chop. Set aside in a large bowl. Powder the fennel seeds, cloves, cinnamon and add to the bowl along with diced onion. Chop the drained lentils in the food processor until smooth enough to make balls. Add this to the bowl along with the salt and mix everything together. Form 1-inch balls, flatten and deep fry until golden brown.

Urid Vada

(Black Gram Lentil Fritters)

Split black gram lentils – 1 cup

Water – ¼ cup

Ginger – 1 tsp grated

Green chili – 1 minced

Black pepper corns – 1 tsp crushed

Curry leaves – 1 tsp chopped

Cilantro – ¼ cup chopped

Oil – for deep frying

Salt – to taste

Method

Soak the lentils for a minimum of four hours. Drain and grind in a food processor with the water. Add the ginger, curry leaves, cilantro, green chili, black pepper, salt and mix well. Form 1-inch balls and flatten on your wet palm. Make a hole in the center and slide into the hot oil and deep fry until golden brown.

Baked Spicy Cabbage

Split chick pea flour – 2 ½ cups
Cabbage – 3 cups chopped
Coconut – ¼ cup grated
Oil – 1/3 cup
Water – 2 cups
Onion – 1 cup chopped
Green chilies – 6 chopped
Ginger – 1 tbsp grated
Cumin – 1 tbsp
Cilantro – 2 tbsp chopped
Salt – to taste

Method

Preheat the oven to 350° F. Mix all the ingredients and pour into a greased oven safe dish and bake for 40 – 50 minutes. Cut into 2-inch cubes.

Charmuri Masala

(Mangalorian Style Spicy Puffed Rice)

Puffed rice – 3 cups

Red onion – ½ cup diced

Cilantro – ¼ cup chopped

Carrot – ¼ cup grated

Sambhar Powder* – 1 tsp

Coconut oil – 1 tsp

Lemon juice – 2 tsp

Salt – to taste

Method

Microwave the puffed rice for 1 minute and set aside. Mix the rest of the ingredients together in a bowl. Mix in the puffed rice just before serving.

* See page 80

Tuna (Fish) Cutlet

Canned Tuna – 1 cup drained and chopped

Peas – ½ cup chopped

Carrot – ½ cup grated

Corn – ½ cup chopped

Onion – ½ cup chopped

Ginger – 1 tbsp grated

Garlic – 6 cloves chopped

Green chilies – 6 chopped

Potatoes – 1½ cups mashed

Cilantro – ¼ cup chopped

Oil – ¼ cup

Egg white – 1 lightly beaten

Bread crumbs – 1 cup

Salt – to taste

Method

Heat 1 tbsp of the oil and sauté the onion. Add chopped garlic, ginger, and green chilies. Stir once and add the tuna, peas, corn and carrots. Sauté on high heat for 3 minutes. Add in the mashed potatoes, salt and cilantro. Remove from heat and cool to room temperature. Form a ball with a heaped table spoon of this mixture. Flatten gently, coat with the egg white first and then with the bread crumbs. Shallow fry the cutlet with the remaining oil until golden brown.

Vegetable Cutlet

Beets – 1 cup grated

Peas – 1 cup chopped

Carrot – 1 cup grated

Onion – 1 cup chopped

Ginger – 1 tbsp grated

Garlic – 6 cloves chopped

Green chilies – 10 chopped

Potatoes – 2 cups mashed

Cilantro – ¼ cup chopped

Oil – ½ cup

Egg whites – 2 lightly beaten

Bread crumbs – 1 ½ cups

Salt – to taste

Method

Heat ¼ cup of the oil and sauté the onion. Add the garlic, ginger and green chilies. Stir and add the beets, peas and carrots. Sauté for 3 minutes. Blend in the mashed potatoes, salt and cilantro. Remove from heat and cool to room temperature. Form a ball with a heaped tbsp of the vegetable mix, flatten gently and coat first with the egg white and then with the bread crumbs. Shallow fry the cutlets with the remaining oil until golden brown on both sides.

Fish Fry

Fish – 4 steaks 1- inch thick of tilapia, salmon, trout or flounder

Red chili powder – 1 tsp

Rice flour – 1 tsp

Mustard powder – ¼ tsp

Cumin powder – ¼ tsp

Oil – 2 tbsp

Salt – to taste

Method

Mix all the powders together and coat each steak. Set aside for at least 15 minutes.

Heat the oil in a nonstick skillet and shallow fry till brown on both sides.

Gojju Avalakki

(Spicy Flaked Rice)

Flaked rice – 2 cups coarsely powdered

Tamarind paste – 1 tsp

Jaggery – 2 heaped tbsp

Curry powder* – 1 tbsp

Peanuts – 1 cup roasted

Curry leaves – 1 tbsp chopped

Turmeric – 1/8 tsp

Mustard seeds – ½ tsp

Split chick peas – 1 tbsp

Split black gram lentils – 1 tbsp

Asafetida – a pinch

Oil – 4 tbsp

Grated coconut – 1tbsp (optional)

Water – 2 cups

Red chilies – 2 broken

Salt – to taste

Method

Bring the water to a boil with the tamarind paste. Add the turmeric, jaggery, curry powder, salt and simmer for 7-8 minutes. Turn off the heat, add the flaked rice and mix well. Cover and set aside until the liquid is absorbed. Heat the oil, and add the mustard seeds. When they splitter, add the red chillies, split chick peas and split black gram lentils. Stir until golden brown. Add asafetida and peanuts. When the peanuts are crisp, add the flaked rice mixture, curry leaves, and grated coconut and mix well.

* See page 79.

Plain Idli

(Steamed Rice Cake)

Rice – 2 cups (Ponni, par-boiled, long-grain)

Split black gram lentils – 1 cup

Water – 2 cups

Salt – to taste

Idli Maker

Method

Soak the rice and the lentils separately for a minimum of 6 hours and drain. Grind the lentils until very smooth and fluffy. Add the rice and continue to blend until the rice is coarsely ground. Salt and ferment in a warm place overnight. Pour the fermented batter into greased idli plates as shown above. Steam for 7-8 minutes. Serve with coconut chutney (page 59), peanut chutney (page 64) or split chick pea lentil chutney (page 65) and/or sambhar (page 48).

Rava Idli

(Steamed Cream of Wheat Cake)

Coarse semolina – 2 cups roasted

Peas – ¼ cup

Carrots – ¼ cup

Cashews – ¼ cup

Curry leaves – 1 tbsp chopped

Cilantro – ¼ cup chopped

Baking powder – ¼ tsp

Mustard seeds – ½ tsp

Oil – 2 tbsp

Yogurt – 3 cups lightly beaten

Salt – to taste

Method

Coarsely chop the peas, cashews and carrots in a food processor and set aside. Heat the oil, add the mustard seeds and let them splitter. Turn off the heat and mix in the chopped ingredients, roasted semolina, salt and baking powder. Stir in the yogurt. Steam in an idli stand for about 7 minutes.

Pav Bhaji

(Indian Style Burger)

Split green gram lentils – 1 cup
Water – 3 cups
Turmeric – ¼ tsp
Green Chili – 1
Pepper corns –- 10
Fenugreek seeds – 10
Cinnamon – 1 stick
Cloves – 4
Red Chilies – 4
Cumin – 1 tsp
Coriander seeds – 1 tsp
Onion – 1 cup diced
Garlic – 1 clove minced
Tomatoes – ½ cup diced
Peas – 1 cup
Cauliflower – 1 cup diced
Carrots – 1 cup diced
Oil – ½ cup and ½ tsp
Cilantro – ¼ cup chopped
Red onion – ¼ cup diced
Butter – for toasting
Buns – 8 round
Juice of 1 lemon or lime
Salt – to taste

Method

Bhaji- Cook the lentils with ½ tsp of oil, a green chili, turmeric and water until done. Roast the pepper corns, fenugreek seeds, cinnamon, cloves, red chilies, cumin, coriander seeds, and powder. Heat the oil and sauté the onions and garlic. Add the vegetables, salt, powdered spices and cook until soft. Mix in the cooked lentils.

To serve, lightly toast the bun by coating with butter. Place a tbsp of the bhaji on the toasted bun and squeeze a little lemon or lime juice over it. Garnish with red onions and cilantro.

Samosa

(Stuffed Vegetable Pastry)

Potato Filling

Potatoes – 3 cups boiled and diced

Ginger – 1 tbsp grated

Peas – 1 cup

Green chilies – 6 chopped

Oil – ¼ cup

Turmeric – ½ tsp

Garam masala powder – 1 tsp

Dry mango powder – ¼ tsp

Cilantro – 1 tbsp chopped

Salt – to taste

Shell

All-purpose flour – 2 cups

Fine semolina – 1 tbsp soaked in tbsp warm water for 5 minutes

Oil – for deep frying and 4 tbsp warm

Salt – 1 tsp

Water – ½ cup warm and about a tbsp for sealing

Method

Heat the oil, add the ginger and green chilies and sauté for 30 seconds. Add the peas, turmeric, garam masala and salt. Sauté for a minute and add the potatoes, dry mango powder, cilantro and mix well. Cool to room temperature.

For the shell, mix the flour, oil, salt and soaked semolina. Drizzle in the water and knead into a soft dough. Let the dough rest for 30 minutes. Form 2-inch balls, roll out into thin circles and cut each circle in half. Form a cone with each half and stuff a heaped tbsp of the potato filling. Seal the edges using a few drops of water. Deep fry until golden brown.

Tandoori Chicken

(Spicy Dry Chicken)

Chicken – 2 lbs or 7 leg pieces slit

Yogurt – 1 cup

Red chili powder – 1 tbsp

Coriander powder – 1 tbsp

Cumin powder – ½ tsp

Vinegar – 2 tbsp

Paprika – 2 tbsp

Oil – 1 tbsp and 1 tbsp to sauté onion

Onion – 1 cup cut into rings

Lemon juice – 1 tsp

Salt – to taste

Method

Mix oil, chili powder, coriander powder, cumin powder, paprika, salt, vinegar and yogurt. Marinate the chicken in this mixture for at least 30 minutes. Bake at 375°F for 45 minutes turning once. Heat the remaining oil in a skillet and sauté the onion rings until soft. Remove from heat, add the lemon juice and salt to taste. Spread over the chicken to garnish.

Plain Upma

(Savory Cream of Wheat)

Coarse Semolina – 1 cup roasted

Water – 3 cups hot

Green chilies – 5 slit

Onion – ½ cup diced

Split chick peas – 1 tbsp

Mustard seeds – ½ tsp

Cilantro – 2 tbsp chopped

Oil – ¼ cup

Salt – to taste

Method

Heat the oil and add the mustard seeds. When they splitter add the split chick pea lentils and green chilies. Stir until the lentils are golden brown. Add the onion. Cover and cook for one minute. Add the water and salt and bring this to a boil. Gently blend in the semolina. Garnish with cilantro.

Khara Bhath

(Spicy Cream of Wheat with Vegetables)

Coarse Semolina – 1 cup roasted

Water – 3 cups hot and ½ cup for cooking vegetables

Oil – ¼ cup

Vegetables – 1 cup each of cauliflower, carrot, potato, green peas,

green beans and eggplant, diced

Vangheebath powder* – 1 tbsp

Mustard seeds – ½ tsp

Onion – ½ cup diced

Cilantro – 1 tbsp chopped

Curry leaves – 1 tbsp chopped

Salt – to taste

Method

Microwave the vegetables with ½ cup water till done. Heat the oil on medium and add the mustard seeds. When they splitter add the onion. Sauté for 2 minutes. Add the 3 cups of hot water, cooked vegetables, vanghee bhath powder, salt and bring to a boil. Stir in the semolina gently on low heat. Garnish with the cilantro and curry leaves.

* See page 81

Usli

(Bengal Gram Salad)

Bengal gram – 2 cups cooked

Ginger – 1 tbsp grated

Onion – ½ cup diced

Green chilies – 6 chopped

Cilantro – 1 tbsp chopped

Asafetida – 1/8 tsp

Mustard seeds – ¼ tsp

Oil – 1 tbsp

Curry leaves – 1 tbsp

Lemon juice – 1 tsp

Salt – to taste

Method

Heat the oil and add the mustard seeds. When they splitter add the ginger, green chilies, asafetida and stir once. Add the onion and sauté lightly. Mix in the cooked beans, curry leaves, lemon juice and salt to taste. Garnish with cilantro.

Aviyal

(Vegetables in a Coconut Sauce)

Vegetables – 1 cup each of diced cauliflower, carrot, green beans, peas and potatoes

Coconut – 4 tbsp

Yogurt – 1 cup lightly beaten

Rice – 2 tbsp

Green chilies – 6

Cumin – 2 tsp

Turmeric – ¼ tsp

Water – ½ cup for cooking and 2 tbsp for grinding

Salt – to taste

Method

Grind the rice, coconut, green chilies, cumin and turmeric with water to a coarse paste. Cook the vegetables with the water and salt in the microwave oven till done. Mix in the ground ingredients with the cooked vegetables and simmer for a minute. Stir in the yogurt. Served with poori or chapati.

Other vegetables often used include chayote squash, drum sticks and winter melon.

Bendekayi Palya

(Okra Stir Fry)

Okra – 5 cups cut length wise

Garlic – 2 cloves crushed

Red chili powder – 1 tsp

Turmeric – ¼ tsp

Cumin powder – 1 tsp

Oil – ¼ cup

Salt – to taste

Method

Heat the oil in a nonstick pan; add the okra and sauté on high heat until okra is done. Mix in turmeric, salt, crushed garlic, cumin powder and chili powder. Serve alone or with chapati.

Cabbage Palya

(Cabbage Stir Fry)

Cabbage – 3 cups thinly sliced

Cumin – 1 tsp

Dry coconut – 1 tbsp

Green chilies – 3 chopped

Oil – 2 tbsp

Mustard seeds – ½ tsp

Cilantro – 1 tbsp chopped

Salt – to taste

Method

Powder the cumin and coconut. Heat the oil and add the mustard seeds. When they splitter, add the cabbage. Stir and add the powdered ingredients, green chilies and salt. Stir, cover and cook on low heat for 5 minutes. Garnish with cilantro. Serve with chapati.

Cauliflower Palya

(Cauliflower Stir Fry)

Cauliflower – 2 cups cut into florets

Onion – ¼ cup diced

Garlic – 1 clove crushed

Oil – 2 tbsp

Mustard seeds – ½ tsp

Curry powder* – 1 tsp

Tamarind paste – ¼ tsp

Eggs – 2 lightly beaten

Turmeric – ¼ tsp

Cilantro – 1 tbsp chopped

Water – 2 tbsp

Salt – to taste

Method

Heat the oil and add the mustard seeds. When they splitter, add the garlic and brown. Sauté the onion until light brown. Add the cauliflower, salt, turmeric, curry powder and tamarind paste. Add the water and cook on high heat until the cauliflower starts to brown. Stir in the eggs and cook until done. Serve with chapati.

* See page 79

Channa Masala

(Garbanzo Beans in a Spicy Tomato Sauce)

Garbanzo beans – 3 cups cooked until soft

Onion – 1 cup diced

Red chilies – 8

Black pepper corns – 1 tsp

Cumin powder – 1 tbsp

Coriander powder – 1 tbsp

Crushed canned tomatoes – 2 cups

Cinnamon – 4 sticks

Cilantro – ¼ cup chopped

Water – 1 cup

Oil – ¼ cup

Salt – to taste

Method

Heat the oil on medium. Sauté the cinnamon, black pepper corns and red chilies. Add the onion and allow it to brown. Add the cumin powder, coriander powder, crushed tomatoes and salt. Cook until the color changes from bright to dark red. Add the cooked beans, water and simmer for 5 minutes. Garnish with cilantro. Served with poori, batoora or chapati.

Egg Curry

Eggs – 8 boiled

Onion – 1 cup sliced

Fresh coconut – 4 tbsp

Coriander powder – 4 tsp

Chili powder – 1tsp

Turmeric – ½ tsp

Tomato – 1 cup diced

Cilantro – ¼ cup chopped

Garlic – 4 cloves

Ginger – 1 inch cube

Cinnamon – 2 sticks

Cloves – 6

Oil – 2 tbsp

Salt – to taste

Method

Grind the garlic, ginger, coconut, turmeric, coriander powder, chili powder, cinnamon and cloves into a smooth paste. Heat the oil and add the onion. Sauté for a few minutes. Mix in the ground paste, salt and cook the paste till brown. Add the boiled eggs, tomatoes and simmer for a few minutes. Garnish with cilantro. Serve with chapati.

Egg Palya

(Egg Stir Fry)

Eggs – 5 without yolk and 1 whole lightly beaten

Onion – ½ cup diced

Mustard seeds – ¼ tsp

Oil – 2 tbsp

Green chilies – 2 sliced

Cilantro – 1 tbsp chopped

Salt – to taste

Method

Heat the oil and add the mustard seeds. When they splitter, add the green chilies, stir and add diced onion. Sauté for 2 minutes. Add the eggs and salt. Stir gently until cooked. Garnish with cilantro. Serve with chapati.

Ennegayi

(Eggplant Stir Fry)

Eggplant – 5 cups slit

Onion – ½ cup sliced

Garlic – 5 cloves

Cinnamon – 2 sticks

Cloves – 5

Green chilies – 5

Ginger – 1 inch cube

Mustard seeds – ½ tsp

Fennel seeds – ½ tsp

Sesame seeds – ¼ cup powdered

Coriander powder – 1tsp

Coconut – ½ cup

Turmeric – ¼ tsp

Curry leaves – 1 tbsp chopped

Cilantro – ¼ cup chopped

Oil – ½ cup

Water – ½ cup

Salt – to taste

Method

Powder the cinnamon, cloves, fennel seeds, coconut and sesame seeds. Finely chop the garlic, ginger and green chilies. Heat the oil and add the mustard seeds. When they splitter, add the chopped ingredients. Stir and add the onion. Sauté and add the eggplant. Mix in turmeric, salt and the powdered ingredients. Cook on high heat stirring occasionally until done. Mix in the curry leaves. Garnish with cilantro. Served with chapati or akki rotti.

Green Beans Palya

(Green Beans Stir Fry)

Green beans – 2 cups finely chopped

Onion – ½ cup diced

Mustard seeds – ½ tsp

Oil – 2 tbsp

Split chick pea lentils – 1 tbsp

Red chilies – 2 broken

Grated fresh coconut (optional) – 1 tbsp

Salt – to taste

Method

Heat the oil and add the mustard seeds. When they splitter, add the split chick peas and stir until golden brown. Add the red chilies, stir and add the onion. Cook for a minute. Add the green beans and salt. Cover and cook until done. Garnish with coconut. Served with chapati.

Green Beans With Lentils

Green beans – 3 cups cut into inch long pieces

Split chick pea lentils – ½ cup soaked and drained

Mustard seeds – ½ tsp

Oil – ¼ cup

Dry red chilies – 3

Asafetida – a pinch

Water – 1 tbsp

Curry leaves – 1 tbsp chopped

Cilantro – 1 tbsp chopped

Salt – to taste

Method

Chop the split pea lentils along with the red chilies and set aside. Microwave the green beans with water until done. Heat the oil in a nonstick pan and add the mustard seeds. When they splitter, add the asafetida, chopped lentils and stir until done. Mix in the cooked green beans, salt and curry leaves. Garnish with cilantro. Serve with chapati.

Heerekayi Palya

(Ridge Gourd Stir Fry)

Ridge gourd – 2 cups finely chopped without pulp

Green Chilies – 3 chopped

Sesame seeds – ¼ cup coarsely chopped

Oil – 1 tbsp

Salt – to taste

Method

Heat the oil and add the chilies. Stir and add the sesame seeds and sauté until golden brown. Add the ridge gourd and cook on high heat until dry. Stir in the salt. Serve alone or with chapati.

Kheema Palya

(Ground Meat Stir Fry)

Ground meat – 1 cup pork, chicken or lamb

Ginger – 1 tbsp chopped

Garlic – 6 cloves chopped

Green chilies – 6 chopped

Onion – ½ cup diced

Oil – 2 tbsp

Coriander powder – 1 tsp

Tomato – ½ cup diced

Corn – ½ cup

Peas – ½ cup

Cilantro – ¼ cup chopped

Salt – to taste

Method

Heat the oil and sauté the ginger, garlic and chili for 30 seconds. Stir in the onion, cook until soft. Add the ground meat. Stir well and cook on high for 5 minutes. Stir in the corn, peas, tomatoes, coriander powder, cilantro and salt. Serve with chapati or poori.

Lamb Chops

Lamb* – 1 lb. with or without bones
Green chilies – 3
Black pepper corns – 1 tbsp
Ginger – 1 inch cube
Garlic – 10 cloves and 2 cloves crushed
Coconut – 2 tbsp fresh or dry
Turmeric – ¼ tsp
Cinnamon – 4 sticks
Cloves – 10
Oil – 1 tsp
Cilantro – ½ cup
Coriander powder – 2 tbsp
Salt – to taste

Method

Finely chop the green chilies, ginger, garlic and cilantro. Powder the coconut, black pepper corns, cinnamon and cloves. Heat the oil and brown the crushed garlic. Add the meat and sauté. Stir in the chopped ingredients, powdered spices and salt. Stir and cook until the meat is tender. Serve with chapati, akki rotti or poori.

*Can also use pork, chicken or goat.

Palak Paneer

(Spinach Curry with Cheese)

Spinach – 1 lb cooked and chopped

Paneer or feta cheese – 1 cup

Tomatoes – 1 cup chopped

Cumin – 1 tbsp

Poppy seeds – 1 tbsp

Ginger – 1 tbsp

Garlic – 3 cloves

Green chilies – 8

Oil – 3 tbsp

Turmeric – ¼ teaspoon

Black pepper corns – ¼ tsp

Salt – to taste

Method

Powder the poppy seeds, pepper and cumin. Finely chop the garlic, ginger, and green chilies. Heat the oil and add the chopped ingredients. Cook for a minute and add the powdered spices. Stir and add the tomato, salt, turmeric and simmer for a minute. Mix in the chopped spinach and bring to a boil. Garnish with paneer. Serve with chapati or poori.

Potato Curry

Potatoes – 2 cups boiled and diced

Green chilies – 6 chopped

Fenugreek powder – ¼ tsp

Fennel seeds – ½ tsp

Turmeric – ¼ tsp

Water – 1 cup

Oil – 2 tbsp

Mustard seeds – ½ tsp

Salt – to taste

Method

Heat the oil and add the mustard seeds. When they splitter, add the green chilies, fenugreek powder and fennel seeds. Stir and add the potatoes, salt, water and turmeric. Simmer for a minute. Serve with masala poori.

Potato Palya

(Potato Stir Fry)

Potatoes – 4 cups boiled and diced

Ginger – 1 tbsp grated

Peas – 1 cup

Green chilies – 6 slit

Onions – 1 cup diced

Oil – ¼ cup

Turmeric – ½ tsp

Garam masala powder – 1 tsp

Mustard seeds – ½ tsp

Cilantro – 1 tbsp chopped

Salt – to taste

Method

Heat the oil and add the mustard seeds. When they splitter, add the ginger, green chilies and sauté for 30 seconds. Add the onions and cook covered until soft. Stir in the peas, turmeric, garam masala and salt. Mix in the boiled potatoes. Garnish with cilantro. Serve with poori or dosa.

Saagu

(Mixed Vegetable Curry)

Vegetables – 1 cup each of diced cauliflower, potato, green beans, squash and carrots

Peas – 1 cup

Fresh coconut – 2 tbsp

Cumin – 1 tbsp

Coriander seeds – 1 tbsp

Roasted split chick peas – 1 tbsp

Green chilies – 6

Water – 1 cup

Milk – ¼ cup

Curry leaves – 1 tbsp

Oil – 2 tbsp

Mustard seeds – ½ tsp

Salt – to taste

Method

Cook the vegetables in the microwave oven with ½ cup water until done. Powder the roasted split chick peas and coriander seeds. Grind the coconut and green chili with milk. Heat the oil and add the mustard seeds. When they splitter, add the cooked vegetables, salt, the powdered ingredients and water. Stir and simmer for a minute. Garnish with the curry leaves. Serve with chapati or poori.

Sambhar

(Spicy Lentils with Vegetables)

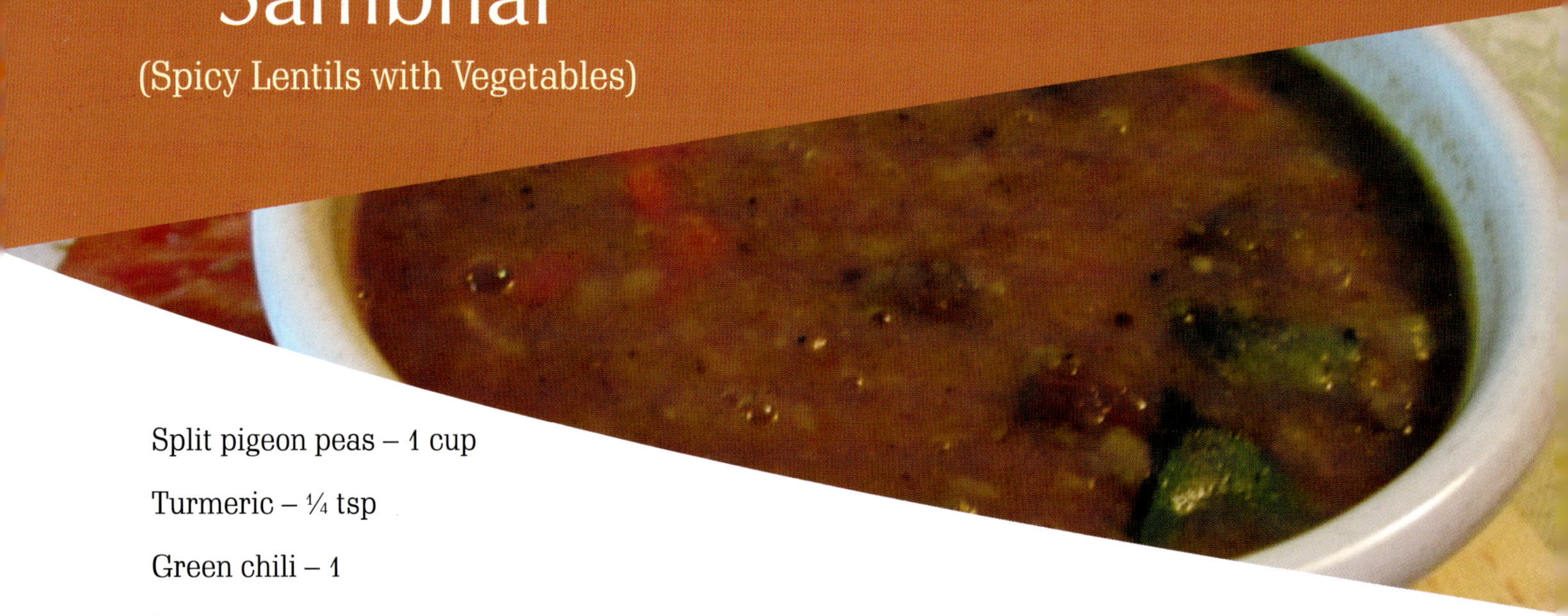

Split pigeon peas – 1 cup

Turmeric – ¼ tsp

Green chili – 1

Water – 3 ½ cups

Carrots – 1 cup diced

Eggplant – 1 cup diced

Tomatoes – ½ cup diced

Tamarind paste – ¼ tsp

Sambhar powder* – 2 tbsp

Coconut – 1 tbsp grated

Oil – 2 tsp

Red Chili – 1

Asafetida – a pinch

Mustard seeds – ½ tsp

Curry leaves – 1 tbsp

Salt – to taste

Method

Cook the lentils with 2 cups of water, green chili and turmeric until soft. Microwave the carrots and eggplant with ¼ cup water until done. Coarsely blend the cooked lentils with the tomatoes, coconut, tamarind paste and sambhar powder. Heat the oil and add the mustard seeds. When they splitter, add the asafetida, red chili, ground lentil mixture and the remaining water. Simmer for a minute and garnish with the curry leaves. Serve with idli.

*See page 80

Thondekayi Palya

(Tindora Stir Fry)

Tindora – 3 cups thinly sliced

Onion – ½ cup diced

Niger seed powder – 1 tbsp

Curry powder* – 1 tsp

Mustard seeds – ½ tsp

Oil – 2 tbsp

Curry leaves – 1 tbsp

Salt – to taste

Method

Heat the oil and add the mustard seeds. When they splitter, add the onion and sauté until light brown. Add tindora and stir fry on high heat for 2 minutes. Lower the heat and mix in the curry powder, niger seed powder, curry leaves and salt. Cover and cook until done. Serve with chapati.

* See page 79

Akki Rotti

(Rice Flat Bread)

Rice flour – 1 cup

All-purpose flour – 2 tbsp

Water – 1 cup

Salt – to taste

Method

Mix all the ingredients into a soft dough. Place the griddle on medium heat. Take a handful of the mixture in the center of the griddle. With a wet palm, spread it in a circle. Cover and cook for about a minute. Flip over and cook for another minute uncovered.

Batura
(Fermented Puffed Bread)

Self-rising flour – 2 cups

Yogurt – 1 cup

Oil – for deep frying and 1 tbsp for coating

Method

Mix the yogurt and flour into a soft dough. Coat with oil and set in a warm place for about 3-4 hours until it rises. Form 2-inch balls, roll and deep fry until golden brown.

Chapati

(Wheat Flat Bread)

Wheat flour – 1 cup

Warm water – 2/3 cup

Rice flour – 2 tbsp for rolling

Oil – 2 tbsp

Salt – a pinch

Method

Mix the wheat flour and salt. Drizzle in the water a little at a time and knead into a soft dough. Form 2-inch balls, flatten and roll using rice flour as needed. Heat a griddle and cook the chapati on both sides. Drizzle oil on the edges before flipping.

Aapam

(Fermented Rice Pancake)

Long grain rice – 2 cups

Flaked rice – ½ cup

Par-boiled or ponni rice – ½ cup

Split black gram lentils – ¼ cup

Baking soda – ¼ tsp

Yogurt – ½ cup

Oil – ¼ cup

Water – ¾ cup

Salt – to taste

Method

Wash and soak the long grain rice, par-boiled rice and split black gram lentils together for 6 hours. Soak the flaked rice separately. Drain and grind the rices with the lentils into a smooth batter by adding water a little at a time. Ferment in a warm place until it rises (approximately overnight). Stir in the baking soda, yogurt, and salt. Place a nonstick griddle on medium heat, pour one large ladle of batter and swirl the pan so that the batter spreads thin on the edges and remains thick in the center. Add ½ tsp oil on the edges. Cover and cook for a minute.

Masala Dosa

(Crispy Rice and Lentil Crepe)

Rice flour – 2 cups

Split black gram lentils – ½ cup

Split chick pea lentils – 1 tbsp

Split green gram lentils – 1 tbsp

Fenugreek seeds – ¼ tsp

Water – 3 cups

Oil for shallow frying – about ¼ cup

Salt – to taste

Method

Soak the lentils and fenugreek seeds for at least 4 hours. Drain and grind finely into a batter adding water a little at a time. Blend in the rice flour and salt adding the remaining water. Ferment overnight. Heat a griddle on medium. Pour a ladle of batter and spread thin. Add a tsp of oil on the edges. Cook for a minute or until golden brown. Serve with coconut chutney (page 59) or split chick pea lentil chutney (page 65) and potato palya (page 46).

Pesarettu

(Green Gram Lentil Pancake)

Split green lentils – 2 cups

Rice – 1 tbsp

Red chilies – 4

Cumin – 1 tsp

Water – 2 cups for grinding

Red onion – ¼ cup finely chopped

Salt – to taste

Oil for shallow frying – ¼ cup

Method

Soak the lentils and rice together for at least 4 hours. Drain and grind along with the red chilies and cumin using about 2 cups of water a little at a time until it reaches pancake batter consistency. Add salt to taste.

Heat a griddle, pour a ladle of batter in the center and spread thin. Drizzle oil over the edges, cover, and cook till golden brown. To serve, sprinkle chopped onion and fold over. Serve with coconut chutney, onion chutney, tomato chutney or split chick pea lentil chutney.

Rava Dosa

(Savory Semolina Crepes)

Fine semolina – 1 cup

All-purpose flour – 1 tbsp

Green chilies – 3 chopped

Red onion – ¼ cup chopped

Cilantro – ¼ cup chopped

Curry leaves – 1 tbsp chopped

Butter milk – 2 cups

Baking soda – ¾ tsp

Oil – ¼ cup for shallow frying

Salt – to taste

Method

Mix all the ingredients except the oil into a pancake batter consistency. Heat a nonstick griddle, pour a ladle of batter and spread thin. Add about a tsp of oil on the edges and cook on both sides until golden brown.

Plain Poori

(Puffed Wheat Bread)

Wheat flour – 2 cups

Water – 1 cup

Oil – for deep frying and rolling

Salt – a pinch

Method

Mix the wheat flour and salt. Drizzle in the water and knead into a firm dough. Roll using a little oil to avoid sticking. Deep fry until golden brown and puffs in the middle.

Masala Poori

(Bread with Lentils and Spices)

Split black gram lentil – ½ cup

Coriander seeds – 1 tbsp

Fennel seeds – 1 tsp

Green chilies – 4

Wheat flour – 1 cup

Water – ½ cup

Oil – for deep frying and 1 tbsp for rolling

Salt – to taste

Method

Soak the lentils for at least 4 hours. Drain and grind with the coriander seeds, fennel seeds, and green chilies. Blend in the wheat flour, salt and knead into a soft dough. Form 1-inch balls, flatten and roll using a little oil to prevent sticking. Deep fry until golden brown. Serve with potato curry or channa masala.

Coconut Chutney

- Coconut – 1 cup grated
- Green chilies – 6
- Ginger – ½ inch
- Yogurt – ½ cup
- Cilantro – ¼ cup chopped
- Pepper corn – ¼ tsp
- Curry leaves – 1 tsp
- Tamarind paste – 1/8 tsp
- Salt – to taste

Method

Grind everything together until smooth.
Serve with idli, rava idli, rotti or dosa.

Date Chutney

Dates – 1 cup pitted

Brown sugar – ½ cup

Tamarind paste – ½ tsp

Water – 1 cup

Method

Add all the ingredients into a saucepan and bring to a boil. Simmer for 5 minutes, cool and blend. Serve with samosa.

Green Chutney

Cilantro – 1 cup

Mint – ½ cup

Green chilies – 2

Cumin – ¼ tsp

Lemon juice – 1 tsp

Salt – to taste

Water – ¼ cup

Method

Grind everything coarsely and serve with pakoda or samosa.

Niger Seed Chutney

Niger seeds – 1 cup roasted

Red chilies – 5 roasted

Tamarind paste – ¼ tsp

Garlic – 2 cloves

Yogurt – 1 cup

Salt – to taste

Method

Blend all the ingredients coarsely. Serve with chapati or rotti.

Onion Chutney

Onion – 2 cups grated

Chili powder – 1 tsp

Mustard seeds – 1 tsp roasted and powdered, 1 tsp for seasoning

Fenugreek seeds – 10 roasted and powdered

Oil – 3 tbsp

Tamarind paste – 1 tsp

Asafetida – a pinch

Turmeric – ¼ tsp

Salt – to taste

Method

Heat oil and add the mustard seeds. When they splitter, add the grated onion and sauté on high heat until the oil starts to separate. Stir in the powdered fenugreek, mustard, turmeric, asafetida, chili powder, salt and tamarind paste. Remove from heat. Serve with chapati, dosa or rotti.

Peanut Chutney

Peanuts – 1 cup roasted and skinned

Red chilies – 5 roasted

Tamarind paste – ¼ tsp

Garlic – 2 cloves

Yogurt – 1 cup

Salt – to taste

Method

Blend all the ingredients coarsely.

Serve with dosa, idli, or rotti.

Split Chick Pea Lentil Chutney

Split chick pea lentil – 1 cup

Ginger – 1 inch cube

Green chilies – 6

Black pepper corn – ½ tsp

Garlic – 1 clove

Coconut – ¼ cup

Cilantro – ¼ cup

Curry leaves – 1 tbsp

Mint – ¼ cup (optional)

Tamarind paste – ¼ tsp

Yogurt – 1½ cups

Salt – 1 tsp

Method

Blend all the ingredients coarsely. Serve with dosa, idli or rotti.

Tomato Chutney

Tomatoes – 3 cups finely chopped

Chili powder – ½ tbsp

Mustard – 1 tsp roasted and powdered and ½ tsp for seasoning

Fenugreek seeds – 10 roasted and powdered

Oil – 3 tbsp

Tamarind paste – ¼ tsp

Asafetida – a pinch

Turmeric – ¼ tsp

Salt – to taste

Method

Heat oil and add mustard seeds. When they splitter, add tomato and stir fry on high heat until the oil starts to separate. Stir in the powdered fenugreek, mustard, turmeric, asafetida, chili powder, salt and tamarind paste and remove from heat.

Besan Laddu

(Split Chick Pea Snack)

Split chick pea flour – 2 cups

Sugar – 1 cup

Ghee – 1 cup

Cashews – ½ cup chopped

Almonds – ¼ cup chopped

Pistachios – ¼ cup chopped

Cardamom – 10 seeded and powdered

Method

Heat 1 tbsp of ghee and roast the chopped nuts and set aside. Heat the remaining ghee add split chick pea flour and stir fry until the color darkens from light to dark yellow (takes approximately 10 – 12 minutes). Mix in the sugar, roasted nuts and powdered cardamom and remove from heat. Let the mixture cool before making 1- inch balls.

Date Burfi

Chopped dates – 2 cups

Almonds – 1 chopped

Pistachios – 1 cup chopped

Cashews – 1 cup chopped

Condensed milk – 1 can

Butter – 2 tbsp

Method

Heat the butter and add the dates. Cook until dates become soft and mushy (2 to 3 minutes). Mix in the condensed milk and keep stirring until it separates from the sides. Remove from heat and add all the nuts. Mix well, cool and kneed the mixture into a long round shape (2 inch diameter) and cut into 1/4 -inch thick slices.

Gulab Jamoon

(Donuts in a Syrup)

Milk powder – 1 1/3 cups

All-purpose flour – 2/3 cup

Baking powder – 2/3 tsp

Butter – 2/3 stick softened

Water – 4¼ cups

Sugar – 2 cups

Rose essence – 2 tsp

Oil – for deep frying

Method

Mix sugar and 4 cups of water together and bring to a boil. Stir in rose essence and set aside. Mix butter, milk powder, all-purpose flour, and baking powder well. Add the remaining water to make a soft dough. Place oil on low heat. Take ½ inch size dough, shape them into round balls and deep fry till they turn golden brown. Put them in sugar syrup when it is still hot.

Kalakand

(Ricotta Cheese Cake)

Ricotta cheese – 2 cups

Condensed milk – 14 oz can

Rose water – 1 tbsp

Butter – 1/8 tsp

Almond pieces – 1 tbsp roasted

Method

Mix ricotta cheese and condensed milk in a large microwavable dish. Microwave at high for 18-20 minutes stirring often. Blend in rose water. Spread on a greased nonstick tray, sprinkle almond pieces and allow the mixture to cool. Cut into pieces and refrigerate.

Karjikayi

(Pastry with Dates and Nuts)

All-purpose flour – 1 cup

Fine semolina – 1 tbsp

Oil – 1 tbsp

Water – 1/3 cup warm

Dates – ½ cup pitted and chopped

Dry coconut – ½ cup grated

Almonds – ½ cup chopped

Cashews – ½ cup chopped

Brown sugar – 2 cups

Raisins – ½ cup chopped

Poppy seeds – 1 tbsp

Cardamom – 6 seeded and powdered

Oil – for deep frying

Method

Soak semolina in warm water. Mix in all-purpose flour and oil to make a soft dough. Mix in cardamom, poppy seeds, chopped raisins, cashews, almonds and dates with brown sugar and coconut. Roll 1- inch ball of dough into round sheets and fill with a heaped tbsp of filling. Fold and seal the edges and deep fry until golden brown on both sides.

Kesari Bhath

(Semolina Pudding)

Coarse Semolina – 1 cup lightly roasted

Sugar – 1¼ cup

Water – 3 cups

Ghee – ½ cup

Cardamom – ¼ tsp

Cashews – ¼ cup cut into small pieces

Raisins – ¼ cup

Saffron – 1/8 tsp

Orange food color – 2 drops

Method

Heat the ghee and lightly brown the cashew nuts and raisins. Add the water, cardamom and food color and bring to a boil. Blend in the semolina slowly stirring until all the liquid is absorbed. Add the sugar and mix well. Cover and cook on low heat for two more minutes.

Mango Kulfi

(Mango Ice Cream)

Heavy Whipping Cream – 1 cup

Mango pulp – 1 cup

Evaporated milk – 1 cup

Sweetened condensed milk – 1 cup

Bread – 2 slices without the crust

Cardamom – 1 tsp powdered

Method

Puree everything together in a blender till smooth. Pour into kulfi moulds and freeze for at least 6 hours until set. Run each mould under running water for 30 seconds to unmould.

Mango Srikhand

(Mango Pudding)

Whole milk yogurt – 8 cups

Sugar – 2 cups

Canned mango pulp – ¼ cup

Almonds – 2 tbsp chopped

Pistachios – 2 tbsp chopped

Cardamom – a pinch

Saffron – a pinch

Method

Strain the yogurt using cheesecloth overnight in the fridge. The volume of the yogurt should reduce by about half. Discard the water; add the sugar and mango pulp to the strained yogurt. Beat until smooth and mix in the saffron and cardamom. Garnish with the nuts. Chill for 4 hours.

Mysore Pak

(Split Chick Pea Cake)

Split chick pea flour – 1 cup

Sugar – 2 cups

Water – 1 cup

Ghee – 2 cups

Method

Prepare the sugar syrup by boiling water with sugar for 5 minutes. In the second pan, place 1 cup of ghee on medium heat, stir in split chick pea flour and fry for 5 minutes. Pour the sugar syrup into the flour and ghee mixture and continue to stir. Add additional ghee 1 table spoon at a time until the mixture turns stringy and pores appear. Empty into a greased container and cut into pieces within 30 minutes.

Badam Milk

(Almond Milk)

Milk – 2 cups hot

Almonds – 2 tbsp skinned

Cashews – 1 tbsp

Sugar – 1 tbsp

Cardamom – 2 seeded

Saffron – a pinch

Method

Finely powder almonds, cashews and cardamom. Stir this into hot milk with sugar and saffron.

It could also be served as cold badam milk by chilling in the refrigerator.

Mango Lassi

(Mango Milkshake)

Yogurt – 2 cups

Sugar – 1 cup

Water – ½ cup

Mango pulp – 1 cup

Salt – ¼ tsp

Method

Blend all the ingredients together until smooth. Chill in the refrigerator before serving.

Masala Chai

(Indian Tea)

2 % Milk – ½ cup

Water – ½ cup

Loose black tea – 1 tsp

Sugar – 1 tsp

Cardamom – 1 seeded

Cinnamon – 1 stick

Ginger – ¼ tsp grated

Black pepper – 1 crushed

Method

Bring all of the ingredients together to a boil. Strain and serve.

Curry Powder

Red chilies – 1/3 cup

Coriander powder – ½ cup

Cumin – 1 tsp

Black pepper corn – ½ tsp

Black gram lentil – 1 tsp

Split chick pea lentils – 1 tsp

Fennel seeds – ½ tsp

Cinnamon – 2 sticks

Cloves – 3

Asafetida – a pinch

Mustard seeds – ¼ tsp

Fenugreek seeds – ¼ tsp

Method

Roast and powder all the ingredients.

Sambhar Powder

Cumin – ¾ tbsp

Coriander seeds – 1½ tbsp

Black pepper corn – 1 tbsp

Red chilies – 3

Fenugreek – ¼ tsp

Method

Roast and powder all the ingredients. Use 2 ½ tsp of this powder for 2 quart of Sambhar.

Vanghee Bhath Powder

Red chilies – 1½ cups

Black pepper corn – ¾ cup

Coriander seeds – 1 cup

Split pea lentils – ¾ cup

Asafetida – 1/8 tsp

Cinnamon – 4 sticks

Cloves – 10

Cardamom – 4

Fennel seeds – 1 tsp

Method

Roast and powder all the ingredients.

Spices and more with alternate names and other details

Ajwain – Carom seeds
Bengal gram – Black chick pea
Besan – Split chick pea flour
Cilantro – Coriander leaves
Flaked rice - Poha
Ghee – clarified butter (melt butter till water gets evaporated. Add a pinch of fenugreek powder and remove from heat).
Jaggery – unprocessed cane sugar
Puffed rice – Murmura
Split black gram - Urid dhal
Split Chik pea lentil – Channa dhal
Split green gram lentil – Mung lentil
Yogurt – Refers to plain yogurt. Unless specified, yogurt is made from 1 or 2 % milk (boil milk and cool milk until luke warm. Stir in a tsp of yogurt and place in a warm area for approximately 6 hours). Results are very similar whether it is homemade or store bought.

Spices & More

Ajwain

Cardomum

Chili Pepper

Cinnamon

Coriander seeds

Cumin

Curry Leaves

Fennel Seeds

Green Gram

Mung

Mustard

Niger Seeds

Poppy Seeds

Roasted Channa

Sesame

Split Pigeon Pea

Urid Dhal

Chaya Gopalan

Chaya Gopalan is a professor of Physiology at St. Louis College of Pharmacy. Besides teaching and research, she enjoys sharing her cooking with friends, family and her students. Dr. Gopalan also enjoys gardening and singing.

Jyothi Kudva

Jyothi Kudva has always been passionate about cooking. When she offered to help write this book, she had no idea how much fun the next six months would be. She fondly cherishes all the meetings, discussions, cooking, photographing, eating and the laughing that took place while working on this book.

Acknowledgments

This book would not have been possible without the support of Keelara Gopalan, Rishub Keelara, Varsha and Shyam Tanguturi, the family members of Chaya Gopalan. Ganesh and Rohan Kudva, the family members of Jyothi Kudva have been very supportive of this project. Sahana Raju was eager to participate in photographing some of the images included in this book. Many of the recipes came from friends and family members and thanks to those who have passed on their talents to others.